To:

From

D1259030

978-1-933494-91-3
Copyright 2009, **Gooseberry Patch**
First printing, June, 2009

Christmas
Classics

Recipes for a
very merry
Christmas.

Gooseberry Patch Cookbooks... they're homemade made easy!

Gooseberry Patch cookbooks are all about friends sharing recipes with friends.

The recipes are easy! They use ingredients that you have in the pantry, they're yummy and they help you get dinner on the table...fast.

Check out our newest titles or start your collection today at **www.gooseberrypatch.com/cookbooks**

Celebration Cheese Ball

2 8-oz. pkgs. cream cheese,
   softened
8-oz. pkg. shredded sharp
   Cheddar cheese
1 T. Worcestershire sauce
1/2 t. salt
1/4 t. celery salt
1 c. chopped pecans
assorted crackers

Blend together all ingredients except pecans and crackers. Cover and chill for 3 hours; form into a ball. Roll in pecans. Keep refrigerated until serving time. Serve with assorted crackers. Makes 8 to 10 servings.

Ring out a holiday greeting to visitors...hang a string of sleigh bells on the front door.

Flaky Sausage Wraps

6-oz. pkg. ground pork
  sausage
1/4 c. onion, chopped
1/4 c. green pepper, chopped
1 clove garlic, minced
1/4 t. mustard

3-oz. pkg. cream cheese,
  softened
1 T. green onion, chopped
8-oz. tube refrigerated
  crescent rolls, separated

Brown sausage with onion, pepper and garlic; drain. Reduce heat; add mustard, cream cheese and green onion, stirring until cheese melts. Cool slightly; place in a food processor. Process until smooth; spread on crescent rolls. Roll up crescent-roll style; arrange on an ungreased baking sheet. Bake at 350 degrees for 10 to 12 minutes. Makes 8.

Appetizer parties are a great way to visit with friends during the busy holiday season. The recipes are so quick & easy to prepare...more time can be spent having fun together.

Pizza Nibblers

1/2 c. oil
1 c. grated Parmesan cheese
20-oz. pkg. pretzel nuggets
1-1/4 oz. pkg. spaghetti
sauce mix

Combine all ingredients in a large bowl; toss to coat nuggets well. Spread nuggets on a baking sheet that has been lined with aluminum foil. Bake for 45 minutes at 275 degrees. Makes 6 to 8 servings.

Winter Wassail

2 c. cranberry juice cocktail
7 c. water
2/3 c. sugar
2 4-inch cinnamon sticks
1 T. whole cloves
1 T. whole allspice
46-oz. can pineapple juice
12-oz. can frozen red fruit
punch concentrate
6-oz. container frozen
orange juice concentrate,
divided

Combine cranberry juice, water and sugar in a saucepan over medium heat. Tie spices in a square of cheesecloth; add to cranberry mixture. Simmer for 20 minutes. Remove from heat; remove and discard spice bag. Stir in pineapple juice, fruit punch and half of orange juice, using remaining half for another purpose. Heat through; serve warm. Makes one gallon.

Use tiered cake stands for bite-size appetizers...so handy, and they take up less space on the buffet table than setting out several serving platters.

Hot Seafood & Artichoke Dip

8-oz. pkg. cream cheese,
  softened
1 c. sour cream
1.4-oz. pkg. vegetable soup
  mix
6-oz. can crabmeat or small
  shrimp, drained

6-oz. jar marinated artichoke
  hearts, drained and
  chopped
1/2 c. red pepper, chopped
Optional: 1/2 t. hot pepper
  sauce

Blend together all ingredients and spread in an ungreased
13"x9" baking pan. Bake, uncovered, for 25 minutes at
375 degrees. Makes 4 cups.

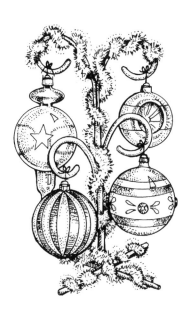

A countertop mug tree makes a fun display rack
for cherished Christmas ornaments.

Garlic Dip

2 8-oz. pkgs. cream cheese, softened
2 T. dill weed
1/2 t. salt
1/2 t. pepper
1 t. dried, minced onion

1/4 onion, chopped
2 to 4 cloves garlic, minced
1 carrot, finely chopped
1 stalk celery, finely chopped
Garnish: paprika
assorted crackers

Combine all ingredients except paprika and crackers, blending well. Sprinkle with paprika. Refrigerate overnight; let stand at room temperature for one hour before serving. Serve with crackers. Makes about 2 cups.

For a magical ice wreath, arrange cranberries and pine trimmings in a ring mold and fill with water. Freeze until solid, then pop out of the mold. Hang outdoors from a tree branch with a sturdy ribbon.

Honey-Glazed Chicken Wings

24 chicken wings   1/2 c. honey
1/2 c. barbecue sauce   1/2 c. soy sauce

Arrange chicken wings in a greased 13"x9" baking pan; set aside. Whisk remaining ingredients together; pour over wings. Bake, uncovered, at 350 degrees for 50 to 60 minutes, or until juices run clear when chicken is pierced with a fork. Makes 2 dozen.

I truly believe that if we keep telling the Christmas story, singing the Christmas songs and living the Christmas spirit, we can bring joy and happiness and peace to this world.

−Norman Vincent Peale

Mushrooms Florentine

16-oz. pkg. mushrooms,
  stems removed and
  chopped
2 T. butter, melted and
  divided
10-oz. pkg. frozen chopped
  spinach, cooked and
  drained
1/2 c. dry bread crumbs
1/2 t. garlic powder
1/8 t. nutmeg
salt and pepper to taste
1/2 c. grated Parmesan
  cheese, divided

Dip mushroom caps into one tablespoon melted butter. Place
in an ungreased 13"x9" baking pan; set aside. In a skillet over
medium heat, sauté mushroom stems in remaining butter.
Remove from heat. Add spinach, bread crumbs, seasonings
and 1/4 cup cheese. Mix well and spoon into mushroom
caps; sprinkle with remaining cheese. Bake, uncovered, at
350 degrees for 20 to 25 minutes. Serve hot. Serves 10 to 12.

Host a giftwrap party...invite guests to bring their gifts
along with rolls of paper to share. Supply tape, tags,
tissue paper, boxes, bows and other festive trimmings.
Play holiday music and serve light refreshments...everyone's
gifts will be wrapped in no time at all!

★ Christmas Classics ★

Maple-Roasted Chicken

6 to 7-lb. roasting chicken
salt and pepper, to taste
1 onion, peeled and cut
    into wedges
1 butternut squash, peeled,
    seeded and cubed

6 carrots, peeled and halved
    lengthwise
3 parsnips, peeled and sliced
2/3 c. maple syrup
2 T. butter

Sprinkle inside of chicken with salt and pepper. Spread vegetables in a deep roasting pan and place chicken on top. In a small saucepan over low heat, mix together syrup and butter until butter melts. Bake at 350 degrees for 2-1/2 to 3 hours, basting with syrup and pan juices. Chicken is done when juices run clear and internal temperature reads 165 to 170 degrees on a meat thermometer. If chicken is browning too fast, cover loosely with aluminum foil. Remove chicken to a large platter; place vegetables around edge of platter. Serves 6 to 8.

For a pretty centerpiece, fill a large, clear glass container
half-full with fresh cranberries. Set a tall pillar candle
in the center of the berries and tuck in holly and greens
around the base.

The Creamiest Mashed Potatoes

5 to 6 potatoes, peeled and
   cut into 1-inch cubes
3-oz. pkg. cream cheese,
   thinly sliced and softened
3 T. butter, softened
4 to 5 T. half-and-half or
   milk

2 cloves garlic, minced
salt and pepper to taste
2 T. fresh chives, snipped,
   or 3 T. dried chives
Garnish: additional butter

Cover potatoes with water in a large stockpot over medium-high heat. Boil potatoes until tender when pierced with a fork, about 15 minutes once they begin to boil. Drain; mash with either a hand masher or an electric mixer on medium speed. Add cream cheese, butter, half-and-half or milk, garlic, salt and pepper. Mix well until cream cheese and butter are melted. Fold in chives; top with a dollop or two of butter. Serves 6.

The more the merrier! Why not invite a neighbor or
a college student who might be spending the holiday alone
to share in the Christmas feast?

Praline Mustard-Glazed Ham

7 to 8-lb. bone-in, smoked
   spiral-cut ham half
1 c. maple syrup
3/4 c. brown sugar, packed
3/4 c. Dijon mustard
1/3 c. apple juice
1/4 c. raisins
1 tart apple, cored, peeled
   and thinly sliced

Remove and discard skin and any excess fat from ham.
Place in a lightly greased 13"x9" baking pan; insert a meat
thermometer in thickest part of ham. Combine syrup, brown
sugar, mustard and apple juice; pour over ham. Set pan on
lowest oven rack. Bake at 350 degrees, basting with drippings
every 20 minutes for 2-1/2 hours, or until thermometer reads
140 degrees. Let ham stand for 10 minutes; remove from pan
to a platter, reserving drippings. Use a bulb baster to remove
and discard fat from drippings. To make sauce, heat drippings
with raisins and apples in a small saucepan over low heat for
5 minutes. Serve sliced ham with warm sauce. Serves 12.

When setting a children's table for Christmas dinner, make it
playful! Cover the tabletop with giftwrap, decorate paper cups
and napkins with holiday stickers and add a gingerbread house
centerpiece...the kids will beg to sit there!

Sweet Potato Crunch

4 sweet potatoes, peeled,
   boiled and mashed
3 eggs, beaten
1 c. sugar
1 c. margarine, melted and
   divided
1/2 c. milk
2 t. vanilla extract
1 c. brown sugar, packed
1/2 c. all-purpose flour
1 c. chopped pecans

Combine sweet potatoes, eggs, sugar, 1/2 cup margarine, milk and vanilla; mix well. Pour into a lightly greased 2-quart casserole dish; set aside. Mix brown sugar, flour, pecans and remaining margarine together; sprinkle on sweet potato mixture. Bake, uncovered, at 350 degrees for one hour. Makes 4 to 6 servings.

A little smile, a word of cheer,
A bit of love from someone near,
A little gift from one held dear,
Best wishes for the coming year...
These make a Merry Christmas!

   -John Greenleaf Whittier

Ziti with Spinach & Cheese

2 10-oz. pkgs. frozen
    chopped spinach, cooked
    and drained
15-oz. container ricotta
    cheese
3 eggs, beaten
2/3 c. grated Parmesan
    cheese

1/4 t. pepper
16-oz. pkg. ziti pasta,
    cooked
28-oz. jar spaghetti sauce
2 t. dried oregano
12-oz. pkg. shredded
    mozzarella cheese

Combine spinach, ricotta cheese, eggs, Parmesan cheese and
pepper; set aside. Combine pasta, spaghetti sauce and oregano;
place half the pasta mixture in an ungreased 13"x9" baking
pan. Layer with spinach mixture and mozzarella cheese. Add
remaining pasta mixture. Cover with aluminum foil and bake
at 375 degrees for 25 minutes. Uncover and bake another
5 minutes, or until bubbly. Remove from oven and let stand
for about 10 minutes before serving. Serves 8.

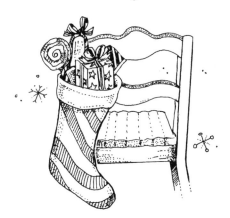

Make grown-ups feel like kids again! Stuff stockings
with penny candy, comic books, card games like "Old Maid"
and other childhood delights...hang from the backs of
dining room chairs with tasseled cords.

Green Beans Amandine

2 T. butter
3 lbs. green beans, trimmed
3 c. chicken broth
1/2 t. pepper
2 T. cornstarch

1/4 c. cold water
2 T. lemon juice
1/4 c. slivered almonds,
  toasted

Melt butter in a large skillet over medium-high heat. Add beans and sauté for 5 minutes. Add broth and pepper; bring to a boil. Reduce heat, cover and simmer for 15 minutes. Dissolve cornstarch in cold water; add to skillet. Bring to a boil; cook for one minute, stirring constantly until thickened. Stir in lemon juice. Sprinkle with almonds. Makes 12 servings.

Cream Biscuits

2 c. all-purpose flour
1 T. baking powder
3 T. sugar

1/2 t. salt
1-1/4 c. whipping cream
Garnish: milk

Combine flour, baking powder, sugar and salt; add cream. Stir mixture until it forms a dough; form into a ball. Knead dough 6 times; roll out 1/3-inch thick on a floured surface. Cut into circles with the rim of a glass; place on an ungreased baking sheet. Brush tops with milk; bake at 425 degrees for 10 to 15 minutes, or until golden. Makes one dozen.

Turn Christmas cards into festive napkin rings. Cut them into strips with decorative-edge scissors, join ends with craft glue and add a sprig of faux holly...simple!

★ Christmas Classics ★

Pineapple-Cranberry Salad

8-oz. can crushed pineapple, drained and juice reserved
16-oz. can whole-berry cranberry sauce

6-oz. pkg. raspberry gelatin mix
1-1/2 c. boiling water

Pour reserved pineapple juice into a 2-cup measuring cup; add enough cold water to equal 1-1/2 cups liquid. Combine cranberry sauce and pineapple; set aside. Dissolve gelatin mix in boiling water; add cranberry sauce mixture and reserved juice. Combine thoroughly and pour into an 8"x8" glass dish. Chill 4 to 6 hours, until set. Cut into squares to serve. Makes 9 servings.

Whip up a batch of drawstring bags in cheery homespun fabric for no-fuss gift wrapping...just pop in a gift and tie the strings in a bow. They'll be reusable year after year too.

Spiced Fruit

29-oz. can sliced peaches
15-1/4 oz. can apricot halves
3/4 c. brown sugar, packed
1/2 c. white vinegar
4 4-inch cinnamon sticks

1 t. whole cloves
1 T. whole allspice
20-oz. can pineapple chunks,
    drained

Drain the juice from peaches and apricots into a large
saucepan; add brown sugar, vinegar and spices, tied in a
square of cheesecloth. Bring to a boil and boil for 5 minutes.
Add pineapple chunks, peaches and apricots to saucepan;
simmer until fruit is warm. Remove and discard spice bag.
Serves 6 to 8.

Place a guest book on the table alongside a jar
filled with colored pencils. Encourage everyone to sign it...
kids can even draw pictures. Add favorite photos
and you'll have a holiday scrapbook in no time!

★ Christmas Classics ★

Cinnamon Pudding Cake

1 c. sugar	2 t. baking powder
2 T. butter, melted	2 t. cinnamon
1 c. milk	1/4 t. salt
2 c. all-purpose flour	

Mix all ingredients together and blend well. Pour into a greased 13"x9" baking pan. Pour hot topping mixture over cake batter. Bake at 350 degrees for 25 minutes. Serves 12.

Topping:

2 c. brown sugar, packed	1-1/4 c. water
2 T. butter	

Combine ingredients in a saucepan over medium heat; bring to a boil.

Dreamy Hot Chocolate

14-oz. can sweetened condensed milk	6 c. boiling water, divided
1/3 c. baking cocoa	Garnish: whipped cream, cinnamon
2 t. vanilla extract	

Combine condensed milk and cocoa in a saucepan; stir over low heat until smooth and warm. Add vanilla and one cup boiling water; mix well. Stir in remaining water. Serve topped with dollops of whipped cream and cinnamon. Makes 6 to 8 servings.

Take the family to a local tree farm and cut your own Christmas tree! Afterwards, warm up with mugs of hot cocoa. You'll be creating sweet memories!

Walnut-Raisin Pie

3 eggs, beaten
2/3 c. sugar
1/2 t. salt
1/2 t. cinnamon
1/2 t. nutmeg
1/2 t. ground cloves

1 c. corn syrup
1/3 c. butter, melted
1 c. walnuts, coarsely
    chopped
2 c. raisins
9-inch pie crust

Beat together eggs, sugar, salt, spices, corn syrup and butter until well mixed. Stir in walnuts and raisins; pour into pie crust. Bake at 375 degrees for 40 to 50 minutes, until set. Serves 6 to 8.

Place newly arrived Christmas cards in a napkin holder, then take a moment every evening to share happy holiday greetings from friends & neighbors over dessert!

★ Christmas Classics ★

Holiday Butter Cookies

2 c. butter, softened
2 c. powdered sugar
4 eggs, beaten
1 t. baking soda

1 t. lemon juice
1 T. milk
5-1/2 c. all-purpose flour

Blend together butter, powdered sugar and eggs in a large bowl;
set aside. Dissolve baking soda in lemon juice; add to butter
mixture. Stir in milk and add flour gradually. Roll dough to
1/4-inch thickness and cut with cookie cutters. Arrange on
ungreased baking sheets; bake at 350 degrees for 8 minutes.
Makes 6 to 7 dozen.

Peppermint Snowballs

18-oz. pkg. chocolate
sandwich cookies, finely
crushed
8-oz. pkg. cream cheese,
softened

6-oz. pkg. white melting
chocolate
1 to 1-1/2 c. peppermint
candies, finely crushed

Mix together crushed cookies and cream cheese. Roll into
1-1/2 inch balls and set aside. Melt white chocolate in the top
of a double boiler over low heat; stir in crushed candy. Dip
balls into chocolate and set on wax paper to harden. Makes
2-1/2 dozen.

Nothing's more fun on a snow day
than building a snowman. Keep a box
filled with all the trimmings...
mittens, scarf, hat and buttons.
Don't forget a camera too!

Gumdrop Jewels

1 c. shortening
1 c. brown sugar, packed
1 c. sugar
2 eggs, beaten
1 t. vanilla extract
1/4 t. salt
1 t. baking powder

1 t. baking soda
2 c. all-purpose flour
1 c. gumdrops, chopped
1 c. chopped nuts
2 c. quick-cooking oats,
    uncooked

Combine shortening, sugars and eggs; beat until smooth. Stir in remaining ingredients. Drop by rounded teaspoonfuls onto ungreased baking sheets. Bake at 350 degrees for 10 to 12 minutes. Makes 2-1/2 to 3 dozen.

A tin filled with favorite Christmas cookies and candies
is extra-special when the recipes are included!

★ Christmas Classics ★

Chocolate Cherry Bars

1/2 c. butter, melted
1-1/2 c. graham cracker
   crumbs
14-oz. can sweetened
   condensed milk

12-oz. pkg. milk chocolate
   chips
10-oz. jar maraschino
   cherries, drained and
   chopped

Spread melted butter evenly in a 13"x9" baking pan. Stir in graham cracker crumbs; press down to form a crust. Pour condensed milk over top; sprinkle with chocolate chips and chopped cherries. Bake at 350 degrees for 25 minutes. Cool completely; slice into bars. Makes about 2 dozen.

Frame something small and sentimental...several of
Grandma's buttons, a tiny mitten, a worn quilt square or
a handwritten recipe. Any of these would make
a heartfelt gift for someone special.

Cranberry-Orange Bread

2 c. all-purpose flour
2 t. baking powder
1/2 t. baking soda
1/4 t. salt
2 t. ground cloves
1 c. sugar

1 c. orange juice
1 egg, beaten
1/2 c. margarine, melted
1 c. cranberries, halved
zest of one orange

Sift together flour, baking powder, baking soda, salt, cloves and sugar; set aside. Blend together orange juice, egg and margarine. Make a well in the center of the dry ingredients and add orange juice mixture to well. Stir until moistened; fold in cranberries and orange zest. Pour into a greased 9"x5" loaf pan. Bake at 350 degrees for 45 minutes, or until a knife inserted in the center comes out clean. Makes one loaf.

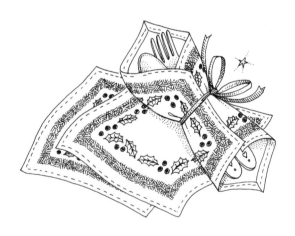

Vintage Christmas napkins can often be found at tag sales...
use them to wrap gifts from your kitchen or
enjoy them on the dinner table!

Santa Cookies

1 c. powdered sugar
2 T. milk
1/2 t. vanilla extract
16-oz. pkg. peanut-shaped
    sandwich cookies
4-1/4 oz. tube red decorator
    frosting

Garnish: quartered mini
    marshmallows, mini
    semi-sweet chocolate
    chips, red cinnamon
    candies

Mix powdered sugar, milk and vanilla together to a frosting
consistency. Spread a small amount of frosting on each end of
cookies, leaving middle of cookies plain to decorate for Santa's
face. Place on a wire rack; let frosting dry completely. Decorate
top of each cookie with red frosting to make a hat. Using white
frosting to attach, add a marshmallow quarter to hat for a
pompom, 2 chocolate chip eyes and a cinnamon candy nose.
Let cookies dry completely on a wire rack before serving.
Makes about 2-1/2 dozen.

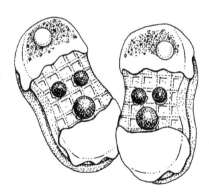

Decorate a mantel with a garland of gingerbread people.
Cut out cookie dough and make a small hole in each "hand"
with a drinking straw. Bake and decorate cookies,
then tie them together side-by-side with narrow ribbon
threaded through the holes.

Reindeer Chow

4 c. salted peanuts
1 c. whole almonds
1 c. candy-coated chocolate
   pieces

1 c. raisins
1 c. chopped dates
1/4 c. shelled sunflower
   seeds

Combine all ingredients in a large bowl; store in a covered container. Makes about 8 cups.

Watch for interesting plates, tins and jars at yard sales.
They're just the thing for delivering food gifts to
friends & neighbors...the recipient will feel extra-special
and the container is theirs to keep.

Maple-Pecan Fudge

3 c. sugar
5-oz. can evaporated milk
3/4 c. butter
12-oz. pkg. white chocolate
    chips

7-oz. jar marshmallow creme
1 t. vanilla extract
1 T. maple flavoring
1/2 to 1 c. pecans, chopped
    or halved

In a large saucepan, mix together sugar, evaporated milk and butter over medium heat, stirring constantly. Bring to a full rolling boil; continue stirring constantly at a full boil for 4 minutes. Remove from heat. Stir in white chocolate chips and marshmallow creme; stir in vanilla and maple flavoring. Add chopped pecans, if using, or wait if using pecan halves. Pour warm fudge into a greased 11"x7" baking pan. If using pecan halves, press into top of fudge. Let set for several hours to overnight; cut into squares. Makes 2-1/2 dozen squares.

Homemade candy is always a welcome gift! Make the gift
even sweeter...place individual candies in mini paper
muffin cups and arrange in a decorated box.

Old-Fashioned Hard Tack

4 c. sugar
1 c. corn syrup
2 c. water
1 t. desired flavoring oil

6 to 10 drops desired food
coloring
Garnish: powdered sugar

Combine sugar, corn syrup and water in a heavy 3-quart saucepan. Cook over medium heat, stirring occasionally, until mixture reaches the hard-crack stage, or 290 to 300 degrees on a candy thermometer. Remove from heat. Carefully stir in flavoring oil and food coloring; pour into a greased 13"x9" baking pan. Set aside on a flat surface until cool enough to remove from pan; cut into 1/2-inch squares or break into pieces. Toss in powdered sugar to coat; store in an airtight container. Makes 2 pounds.

Too sweet...wrap packages in plain red wrapping paper and glue a row or two of wrapped red & white peppermints all across the top.

Nifty Gifty
CARDS & TAGS

Be Merry!

JINGLE BELLS

PEACE · Let it Snow!

Have a Merry Christmas

JOY

Write the recipe on the back!

HAPPY HOLIDAYS!

From the kitchen of:

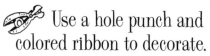
Use a hole punch and colored ribbon to decorate.

1. CopY 2. Color 3. Cut Out!

Warm Wishes

INDEX

Enjoy these favorites from our
***Gooseberry Patch** hardcover cookbooks!*

INDEX

Gooseberry Patch
cookbooks

Since 1992, we've been publishing our own country cookbooks for every kitchen and for every meal of the day! Each title has hundreds of budget-friendly recipes, using ingredients you already have on hand in your pantry.

In addition, you'll find helpful tips and ideas on every page, along with our hand-drawn artwork and plenty of personality. Their lay-flat binding makes them so easy to use...they're sure to become a fast favorite in your kitchen.

Send us your favorite recipe!

and the memory that makes it special for you!* If we select your recipe for a brand-new **Gooseberry Patch** cookbook, your name will appear right along with it... and you'll receive a FREE copy of the book!

Submit your recipe on our website at
www.gooseberrypatch.com

Or mail to:

Gooseberry Patch • Attn: Cookbook Dept.
2500 Farmers Dr., #110 • Columbus, OH 43235

*Please include the number of servings and all other necessary information!

 Our Story

Back in 1984, we were next-door neighbors raising our families in the little town of Delaware, Ohio. Two moms with small children, we were looking for a way to do what we loved and stay home with the kids too. We had always shared a love of home cooking and making memories with family & friends and so, after many a conversation over the backyard fence, **Gooseberry Patch** was born.

We put together our first catalog at our kitchen tables, enlisting the help of our loved ones wherever we could. From that very first mailing, we found an immediate connection with many of our customers and it wasn't long before we began receiving letters, photos and recipes from these new friends. In 1992, we put together our very first cookbook, compiled from hundreds of these recipes and, the rest, as they say, is history.

Hard to believe it's been over 25 years since those kitchen-table days! From that original little **Gooseberry Patch** family, we've grown to include an amazing group of creative folks who love cooking, decorating and creating as much as we do. Today, we're best known for our homestyle, family-friendly cookbooks, now recognized as national bestsellers.

One thing's for sure, we couldn't have done it without our friends all across the country. Each year, we're honored to turn thousands of your recipes into our collectible cookbooks. Our hope is that each book captures the stories and heart of all of you who have shared with us. Whether you've been with us since the beginning or are just discovering us, welcome to the **Gooseberry Patch** family!

JoAnn & Vickie

Visit our website anytime
www.gooseberrypatch.com

Join
Our Circle of
Friends

Find us on
Facebook

Follow us on
twitter

1•800•854•6673

Made in the USA
Lexington, KY
14 July 2015